D0873483

Keeping Love Alive

Inspirations for Commitment

Tian Dayton

Health Communications, Inc.
Deerfield Beach, Florida

Publisher: Health Communications, Inc.
          3201 S.W. 15th Street
          Deerfield Beach, Florida 33442-8190

Cover design by Andrea Perrine Brower
Cover illustration: Lovers: *Sir Edward Burne-Jones*
Courtesy of Robin Hubbard

Dedication

To Brandt

my friend
my lover
my partner
in life

may we live
together
one hundred
autumns

Teen

We must be our own before we can be another's.

Emerson

MY GARDEN

A relationship has a life of its own. It exists in the space between two individuals and is fed by those people. Like a garden, it is a growing thing and needs to be tended. What is sown is what will grow and the quality of nurturing will reveal itself in the health of what comes forth. There will be storms, forces of nature that will visit their destruction on the garden; sometimes it will seem as if the entire acre needs to be redug, resown and grown anew. At these times I will remember that this ground is sacred to me. It is the earth that I have loved and tended for years that has fed me and brought me pleasure. It is my little plot, a part of my life and heart. I will dig my hands deep into this soil, into this relationship, and I will look for life. When the storms come, I will remember the fruit, and when the fruit comes, I will remember the storms. If my relationship is alive, it is subject to the elements.

I have spread my dreams beneath your feet;
Tread softly because you tread on my dreams.

W. B. Yeats

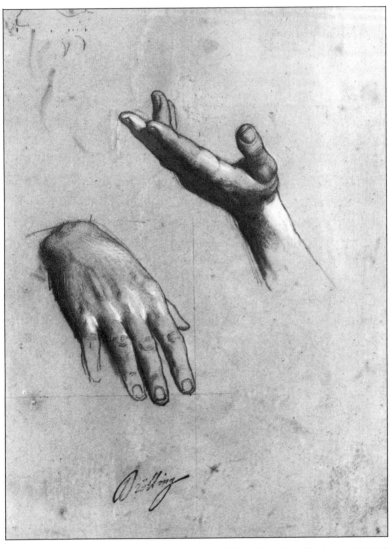

Study of Hands

Martin Drolling, (Paris 1752-1817)

HAVING A SELF

I do not need to give up having a self in order to have a relationship in my life. Having a self is crucial if I am truly going to have a partnership in which I am more than an extension of another person. Maintaining a sense of self is an inside job. It is not about what I do or don't do but how I feel about myself. If I see myself as dependent for my own activities and identity on another person, I will be constantly waiting for permission to follow my own path. If I wait for someone else to tell me what my plans are, I lose my ability to dream my own dreams and walk into my own day. The only way I can feel good about another person or comfortable letting them have a self is if I allow myself to have one too. It is from this place that I can truly love.

Happiness comes more from loving than being loved;
and often when our affection seems wounded, it is only our
vanity bleeding. To love, and to be hurt often, and to
love again — this is the brave and happy life.

S. E. Buckrose

3

THE NOW

I will experience the here and now of our relationship. What is happening is what is. We do not exist in a separate reality but in one that functions from day to day. Who we are in our minute-to-minute interactions is a mirror on the surface of the water reflecting the depths of all that we are. The moment is important. It is the palette that I hold in my hand with which we paint our portrait. It is the clay, the film, the pen and paper, it is our substance with which we create our very being. I will not waste the moment.

When you love someone . . . you do not love him or her in
exactly the same way, from moment to moment. It is an impossibility.
And yet this is exactly what most of us demand. We have
so little faith in the ebb and flow of life, of love,
of relationships. We leap at the flow of the tide and resist
in terror its ebb. . . . The only real security in a relationship
lies neither in looking back in nostalgia, nor forward
in dread or anticipation, but living in the present
relationship and accepting it as it is now.

Ann Morrow Lindbergh

AS YOU ARE

Over the years I have grown to know you, to appreciate you as you are. To love you not for who I thought I wanted you to be but for who you are. This is the greatest gift I can give to you and the most precious one I can receive. To love and be loved as we are. I will walk beside you. Our steps in time, our steps out of time. Walking over the same path in different ways, each at our own pace.

When love beckons to you, follow him.
  Though his ways are hard and steep.
And when his wings enfold you,
    yield to him.
Though the sword hidden
    among his pinions may wound you.
And when he speaks to you,
    believe in him.
Though his voice may shatter your dreams
    as the north wind
    lays waste the garden.

Kahlil Gibran

MEETING NEEDS

*B*ecause I have learned to iden-
tify my needs does not mean that I will hold you responsible
for meeting them. My needs are my own and it is up to me to
see that they are met in a variety of ways. When I look to you
to meet too many of them, I create a lopsided life for myself
and a kind of co-dependency that is not good for either of us.
There are many basic needs that you meet for me just by being
my partner in a steady, reliable relationship. When those basic
needs are well met, the rest of life looks different. I will attempt
to be reasonable in what I expect from you and likewise reasonable in what I expect from myself. Holding each other responsible for one another's needs is a breeding ground for
resentment and a never-ending job. I will realistically assess
what I get from you that really counts at a deep level and then
look at what is fair to expect and give from there.

Seldom, or perhaps never, does a marriage develop
into an individual relationship smoothly and without crises;
there is no coming to consciousness without pain.

Carl Gustav Jung

Tete d'Homme les mains Croisees sur la Poitrine

Alphonse Henri Perin
(Paris 1798-1874)

EXPLORING MY SHADOW

I will explore my own shadow self. My shadow is an enormous part of who I am. When I refuse to see and know significant parts of me, I unconsciously project those feelings onto other people. When I will not own the part of me that feels unlovable, I create circumstances in life that "prove" to me that I am unlovable. I draw people and situations to me that help make my repressed feelings conscious. My mind has a natural wish to know itself and it will seek to bring forward repressed material, either into the healthy light of understanding or the convoluted form of feelings that I project onto another person or situation, then quickly disown. I will take a risk today and feel my most painful feelings, even if I want to run from them. I know this will clean out my insides so that I can make room for more serenity and inner peace. I will look first at myself.

As I was going up the stair
I met a man who wasn't there.
He wasn't there again today.
I wish, I wish he'd stay away.

Hughes Mearns

MAKING A MESS

An artist with a disheveled studio or a writer with a basket full of crumpled paper may feel that chaos is a crucial part of the creative process. In the same way, I am willing to make a mess in our relationship as part of our creative life-giving process. How can we go from numbness to life, from stagnation to spontaneity or from boredom to pleasure without passing through a period of confusion and instability? If we choose life rather than the status quo, we will have to search out our own answers. If we only play roles and forget to look into each other's hearts and eyes and know one another, we are not truly tasting the banquet before us. There is so much about you that I would like to come to know better and keep company with. I deeply appreciate all that you mean to my life, and I wish to allow you the freedom to explore yourself in my presence. This is a gift that benefits both of us. In giving you space to expand beyond your roles, I also am the benefactor of that space. I give us both room to be.

The most beautiful thing we can experience
is the mysterious. It is the source of
all true art and science.

Albert Einstein

BONDING

I am bonded to you by what cannot be seen. By the thousands of hours we have passed in pleasure. The countless small encounters. All of your complaints that I have listened to and my tears that you have wiped away. I am bonded to you by our companionable silence, by the endless details that we know about each other. The bond that is between us is deeper than I am conscious of. It reaches into places that I forget are there. I will not undervalue or underestimate what it means to my life, my heart and my psyche to have this type of ongoing bonding experience. Replicating it would be no easy task and eliminating it would be impossible. It is a part of me forever. Respecting it and nurturing it are what will keep it growing and alive.

If you press me to say why I loved him,
I can say no more than it was because
he was he and I was I.

Montaigne

BEING RIGHT

*B*eing right used to seem so much bigger with you than it does now. I used to feel if I lost ground that I was giving up something very important. I can't remember now what it was that I was afraid of losing. Today I know that each of us has our own truth or way of seeing a situation that is right for us. If I try to take away your sense of what feels right to you and make you live with my sense of the situation, it doesn't fit for you. If I allow your visions and definitions of life to drive me and tell me who I am, it doesn't fit for me. Each of us needs to be with our own experience first and then share it with the other. That is ultimately what will provide us with a sense of security, self and communion. Relationships are not about cloning but about sharing. If communication is prescripted by either party or society at large, we'll never plumb our own depths. How then can we bring depth to our relationship?

A good marriage is like a good trade.
Each thinks he got the better deal.

Ivern Ball

Portrait of a Family   *Ange Francois (Brussels 1810)*

HISTORY

When I was young, I grew up in the environment of my parents' relationship. I imprinted what I saw at a very young and deep level. What I imprinted remains stored in my brain as my own personal "how to" archive on couple behavior. How my parents handled situations from family meals, money, in-laws, is how I was taught by example to handle them. What came easily to my parents often comes easily to me and what was difficult for them can be difficult for me as well. I will ask myself when I have relationship problems if I am living in the present or acting out what was going on with my parents at that particular stage of their relationship. Am I repeating what they would have done in that situation whether or not it is appropriate now? If the answer is "yes," I have some work to do. I will survey from where I stand. My circumstances are vastly different from those of my parents.

From the moment of his birth the customs into which
(an individual) is born shape his experience and behavior.
By the time he can talk, he is the little
creature of his culture.

Ruth Fulton Benedict

BEING ENOUGH

Today I will work to maintain a sense of self within the context of our relationship. I am so quick to organize my insides and outsides according to what I imagine you would like me to be. By doing this I enter into a mythical relationship with people neither of us know or can know because they are constructions of dreams and fantasies rather than the real McCoy. When I try to change myself to suit what I perceive to be your wishes and desires, the next person I want to change is you. I consider it the appropriate trade-off and when you do not or cannot change, I grow disappointed and disillusioned. I rob myself of the experience of us and of being with myself as I am and grow fearful of discovering a hidden you. I become fear driven in our togetherness, silently waiting to be found out for who I really am. I need to trust that who I am will be enough for me and enough for you.

They were upon their great theme:
"When I get to be a man!" Being human, though boys,
they considered their present estate too commonplace to be
dwelt upon. So, when the old men gather, they say:
"When I was a boy!" It really is the land of
nowadays that we never discover.

Booth Tarkington

TAKING CARE OF OUR RELATIONSHIP

*I*n this world of object worship and me-first living, I will not lose my head and forget that the real riches in life are relationships. Taking care of myself first does not mean that I have a right to forget that you have feelings also. If I take care of myself in a way that does not take your humanity into account, I am training you to treat me that same way. I am just giving selfishness a new name and face. Once again I am doing something that sounds good but feels bad. When taking care of myself means that I shove your insides aside, I will remember what it feels like to have that done to me. I will keep in mind that I am an equal partner with you and that there is such a thing as taking care of that partnership as well as myself. There is a way to take care of myself as a separate person within my relationship without forgetting that the relationship also needs to be considered.

A lady of forty-seven who has been married
twenty-seven years and has six children knows what love
really is and once described it for me like this:
"Love is what you've been through with somebody."

James Thurber

COMPROMISES

hings will not go the way that I want them to in our relationship. I will need to adjust, to find a balance between giving up enough so that I am fair to you but not so much that I am not fair to myself. Compromise is not a dirty word and when it is done well, there is great freedom in it for both sides. When I can compromise successfully, it means that I am able to look at both the self and the other with equal value. I am willing to see that another person has the same inner makeup as myself. This makes me feel less alone in the world and more understood, not only because I have extended these things to myself, but because I have also given them to another. The giving and receiving is all the same. The understanding I show to another person automatically returns to me from somewhere because that channel is open within me. The on/off switch is always in my own hands.

Seek not so much to be understood
as to understand.

St. Francis of Assissi

16

BEING DIFFERENT PEOPLE

When I feel my own
    feelings and let you feel
    yours,
It does not necessarily mean
    that we will not get
    along.
You are not here to satisfy
    my needs.
What I did not get is not up
    to you to supply.
Your job is not to finish up
    my insides
Or to be hostage to the
    deficits of my past.
What you give me you give

Because at some deep level
Our needs speak to one
    another.
We call out in the silence
Of our unfinished selves,
To grow through one
    another's
    gifts and desires.
We cannot but serve each
    other's
Inner movement,
    if we allow the
    unconscious match
    between us to do its
    work.

OUR LOVE

Our love has a purpose of its own. It shelters us from the elements. It is a shared experience, a feeling that surrounds, something deep that is generated between us. It can be felt by ourselves and others. It heals. It makes ordinary time pass in a quiet kind of beauty. It allows. It defines. It motivates. Our love does not have boundaries and yet it sets limits through its caring. It stretches me beyond myself. It connects us with something that is larger than either of us. It anchors us in the world. Our love for each other teaches us to reach beyond our own selfishness in search of generosity. When we feel there is no hope and cannot think of another possible way to look at a problem, it opens an unexpected door. It teaches us to wait and spurs us on to action. It is something worth taking care of, worth fighting for. Our love gives meaning and truth to our lives.

I call "crystallization" that action of mind
that discovers fresh perfection in its
beloved at every turn of events.

Stendhal

Nymphe et Zephyr   *Camille Bellanger (Paris, 1853-1923)*

RESOLVING CONFLICT

We do not need to resolve all of our conflicts. Hearing each other out and acknowledging that each of us has a right to our own truth is often enough. If resolving things means seeing eye to eye or somehow ending up with the same point of view, we could spend our lives at it and still never feel satisfied. Because we are in a relationship together does not mean that we own each other's inner reality. I am not with you to collect on an invisible debt or get you to sign on the dotted line. I am here to enjoy your companionship and the support of your presence in my life. Working out conflicts involves a lot of hearing each other share our own truth in a considerate and responsible manner without blame, insult or projection. When we can leave the blame out and talk about our own fears, anxieties and concerns, our discussions become more positive and constructive and we reach a place of feeling good much more quickly.

If we could read the secret history of
our enemies, we should find in each man's life
sorrow and suffering enough to
disarm all hostility.

Henry Wadsworth Longfellow

PLEASURE

I will remember the importance of enjoyment — spending lots of time in easy, pleasant recreation. This is the art of living. Relaxing with a cup of tea, savoring a delicious dinner, taking a walk. Really the world is here for us to enjoy — not to identify with, possess, control and own, but to experience. What is the use of prosperity if we do not take time to enjoy life? What is the point of owning things if they do not bring us pleasure? What we share in this way bonds us at an important level. Little pleasures accumulate and provide a sense of deep contentment. They allow something down inside of us to relax and let go. They abide within as a connection to each other and to life.

Gather ye rosebuds while ye may
Old time is still a-flying
And this same flower that smiles today
Tomorrow will be dying.

Robert Herrick

GRANTING SPACE

I will let you be you and me be me. My efforts to make us alike so that I do not have to suffer my fear of abandonment simply won't work. It is okay to be different. In fact, it is unavoidable. I cherish the space between us, walking side by side without touching — being in the same house each in a different room. Your presence in silence acts on me like a warm, summer afternoon. You have your own Higher Power and I have mine. I will not seek to be yours nor will I allow you to act as mine. If, at times, we drop each other, I will trust life to hold us up.

Love one another, but make not a bond of love:

Let it rather be a moving sea between the shores of your souls.

Fill each other's cup but drink not from one cup.

Give one another of your bread but eat not from the same loaf.

Sing and dance together and be joyous, but let each one of you be alone.

Even as the strings of a lute are alone though they quiver

with the same music.

Give your hearts, but not into each other's keeping.

For only the hand of Life can contain your hearts.

Kahlil Gibran

COMPETITION

Why do I find fault with you? You are not the cause or cure of my life. Living with you is just living with you. When I look to you to solve my own life, I doom our relationship from the start. You are busy enough solving your own life. When I constantly complain about you in my mind, I set up a dynamic between us, in our home and inside my mind. I am not in competition for a self. My relative size to someone else does not define who I am. There is enough space in our relationship for each of us to have an identity. An identity is not something we share — we each need our own. It is all right for me to be my natural size, to go in whatever direction feels right to me. Stifling my own spontaneity and creativity in an effort not to appear overbearing only builds up resentment inside me, and then, inevitably, I will take it out on you.

You can end love more easily than
you can moderate it.

Seneca

Apotheosis of Napoleon I   *Jean Auguste Dominique Ingres (Paris, 1780-1867)*

BEING MYSELF

Once I thought intimacy meant that we knew all about one another, that I lived inside of another person's skin and had rights from that position. I thought that to understand them meant to finish their sentences for them rather than to let them finish their own. I felt that to be close to someone meant signing away my own rights to individual personhood. I didn't know that I could be an individual with my own feelings and remain cared for even if what I thought and felt differed from those I loved. I thought that to be loved I had to please.

I will not expect so much of love today either from me or from you. When I expect love between each other to look a certain way — my way — I get into trouble. It is then hard for me to accept you as you are if you are not doing what I want you to do. How much of this is my need for control? Where does it get me to exert that control over you? There is nothing that says that I have to like or approve of all that you do nor you of me. We each can be individuals with our own ways of being.

According as the man is, so much you honor him.
Terence

INNER SEARCH

Today I recognize that my life is lived through no one but me. I am the source of sustenance and strength that I am looking for. Within me lies all the beauty, strength and wisdom it will take to create a self. I am my own best friend and my beacon in the storm. My light lives within and I am the keeper of my own flame. I do not need to wait to be granted a self from some outside source. I will be the grantor. Accumulating accolades from outside in an attempt to establish an inner identity will not accomplish what I am hoping for. They will just offer me more lessons in what I am not. Ultimately I will need to locate myself from within; the soul that I search for, I already have.

Belinda: *What did you learn?*

Dorothy: *I learned that if I ever lose my heart's desire again, I won't go looking past my own backyard — because if it isn't there, I never really lost it to begin with. Is that it?*

Belinda: *That's all it is.*

L. Frank Baum

Seated Male Academy

Charles Andre Van Loo (Paris, 1705-1765)

PUTTING MYSELF FIRST

I realize that to let myself be first in my life is actually the way of the spirit. Each of us is connected to God through our higher selves. Only from the place of my higher self can I truly be with another person. When my focus is constantly on another, rather than "be" with them I "become" them, and we enter into a sort of competition for one life, one self. My self is the place from which I operate. There is nothing holy about relinquishing it. The way to be generous is to expand or extend myself — not to give my self away. There is a way of first checking in with myself that can actually become less selfish. The question to ask is not what I want vis-a-vis another person, but how I am feeling inside at this moment. When I center in the moment, I see things differently. I take care of myself by living from a centered place within me where I am in touch with my own spirituality and inner wisdom. It is not so much about what I do but where I am within my own being.

> *This above all: To thine own self be true,*
> *And it must follow as the night the day*
> *Thou canst not then be false to any man.*
>
> *Shakespeare*

FORGIVENESS

I will search out the light in your eyes and the love and forgiveness in your heart. If I loved you once, how can I forget that it is possible? Over and over and over again we will need to forgive one another. When I nurture rancor and resentment in my heart, it suffocates the love that I am capable of feeling for you. Everything between us cannot always be resolved. Some of our conflicts need to be let go of in what will feel like an unfinished state. We two are different. Why should we be able to work out each and every difference that we have? I can hear you and you can hear me out. I can respect your right to your point of view and feelings and you can respect mine. Changing you to think and feel like me or changing me to think and feel like you is not what it's all about. Forgiveness comes more easily when I understand that we each have our own path in life.

And all throughout eternity I forgive you
and you forgive me.

W. B. Yeats

I HAVE A RIGHT TO FEEL GOOD

I have a right to be happy whether or not our relationship is going well. Our relationship exists outside of me and will go through many deep changes over the years. If I will not allow myself to feel good, satisfied and successful until our relationship is just right, I am in trouble. How many days of the week will our relationship be "just right," and what will it do to me and to you to postpone my peace of mind until we get it there? Our relationship does not define me. I have a right to feel good about myself in the privacy of my own heart, regardless of what is going on with us. When I make feeling good about myself dependent on how we are doing, I try to control you so I can feel good about me. I force solutions before the time is right and create more stress. I will give us each space to feel our own feelings. I will let go.

One of the signs of passing youth is
the birth of a sense of fellowship with other
human beings as we take our place among them.

Virginia Woolf

COLLUSION

Collusion is not closeness. If I indenture myself to you by pleasing you in silent fear of losing you, I will lose you anyway. Not by your departure but by my own. Even if you stay with me, I will not be there. The silent agreements we make to give wounded parts of ourselves to each other, in the hope that they will somehow be fixed, create blind spots in our relationship. Eventually, though, pain eats its way through our isolation and makes us feel strangers in each other's presence. I will see all of you and let you see all of me.

Losing myself in you would not be wise. When I go to look for myself, you may experience it as an invasion of your privacy, an intrusion into your insides. If I let myself be lost in you, I will come to regard you as a thief. There is a way for me to love you fully without relinquishing myself in service of that love. It involves a sense of self-respect, a knowledge of boundaries and an understanding that people are not possessions. It is knowing where I stop and you begin, trusting that we are joined at the heart rather than at the hip. We can allow each other freedom of movement without losing one another.

Love does not cause suffering:
What causes it is the sense of ownership,
which is love's opposite.

Antoine de Saint-Exupery

Still Life With Book and Olive   *Marcellin Desboutin*

LIVING

You need no longer fulfill
my dreams of a life. That would not be fair.
It never worked anyway.
Have dreams of your own. Dream them in the privacy
of your own mind and let your imagination talk to
your spirit and move forward into more of you.
Have a cup of tea with me.
You need no longer step in time while I call out
the beats.
Find the beat that is right for you and move to it.
Let your body lead you into places you have
not gone as yet.
Take a walk with me.
You need no longer explain my life to me, I will explain
it to myself. I will formulate my own questions and
search out the answers in the quiet of my
own heart.
Let's chat a while.
You need no longer breathe life into my lungs. I will
draw my own breath from the infinite supply
available to me always — there patiently waiting.
Touch my hand,
brush up against me,
kiss my lips.

MODELING

What do I see when I look at my parents' relationship and how does that shape my thoughts, feelings and behavior? I had no greater teachers than my own parents. What I experienced growing up in the cradle of their partnership formed my understanding of relationships. What do I see when I look at my siblings, my grandparents, my aunts and uncles? What have these people taught me about what relationships can mean in my life and how to go about having them? What did I learn when I was young from my peers about how I fit in a group? The models that I grew up with were my relationship teachers. They, by example and interaction, showed me what relationships were all about and how I should conduct myself within them. What I saw as possible for them may be what I feel is possible for me. In what ways have the lessons I learned from them, both positive and negative, translated themselves into how I live inside my relationships today?

Most of the problems a president has to face
have their roots in the past.

Harry S. Truman

KEEPING MYSELF

*I*f I wish to feel good about my life, I need to see it as my own. Too often I give myself away to whomever will have me. Unfortunately when I give my own life away, I want another in return to fill the void. If I find myself excessively preoccupied with another person — even living in their skin — rather than ask myself what parts of them I wish to own, I will ask myself what parts of myself I have given away. How much of my autonomy have I turned over to another person without even being asked? Really maturing as a person is to take one's day into one's own hands and enter into it with full ownership and energy. This is my day to co-create with a Higher Power, to live, engineer and appreciate. I am responsible for my day.

When you have shut your doors and darkened your room,
remember, never to say that you are alone;
for you are not alone,
but God is within, and your genius is within.

Epictetus

DARKNESS

I embrace the darkness within me. What I deny about myself grows in strength and power. I befriend and love that about me which I have designated as unlovable. Just as I feared the darkness in my room as a child, today I fear the darkness in the depths of my being. If I can learn to embrace this part of myself and even love it, I am giving it the opportunity to transform or transmute into another state — to change its level of vibration. I can do more to alter my experience of life by loving the unlovable in myself than by finding reasons to keep it in hiding. When I do not run from what I fear in myself, you do not frighten me so much. The inner strength that I gain from self-knowledge and acceptance finds its way into the arena of our relationship.

When is death not within ourselves? . . .
Living and dead are the same, and so are awake and
   asleep, young and old.

Heraclitus

Untitled   *Aloys Wach (Munich, c. 1917)*

COMPLETION

You are not here to fulfill my fantasies or be the person who will make me feel complete. I need to feel complete all on my own. We shape one another in subtle and not so subtle ways by our presence in each other's lives. We need to remember that we also have to shape ourselves. For me to shape myself according to what I perceive to be your expectations of me would be a loss to both of us. To me because I would deprive myself of a sense of becoming and feel less and less connected with my own insides. To you because you would lose the person you fell in love with. Two would-be people make one would-be relationship. Somehow I don't think it would have the lasting power that two real people coming together in honesty might have.

The jailer is another kind of captive.
Is the jailer envious of his prisoner's dreams?

Gerard de Nerval

WE TOUCH AT POINTS

I will not necessarily agree with all that you say. Why should we as two adult people have to see eye to eye before we can feel comfortable in each other's presence? There is room enough for separate, if not diverging, points of view. Before I blindly accommodate, I will first take my own counsel. Too often when I force myself to be compliant, resentment builds up underneath. We touch at points, you and I. I cannot grow in your shadow nor you in mine. I will not think that by sheltering you from me or me from you, I am helping either of us. Rather I will grow beside you and let you grow beside me resisting the urge to hang on too tightly at the root. I will let you take in a full breath of you and I will take in a full breath of me.

All paths lead to the same goal: To convey to others what we are. And we must pass through solitude and difficulty, isolation and silence, in order to reach forth to the enchanted place where we can dance our clumsy dance and sing our sorrowful song — but in this dance or in this song there are fulfilled the most ancient rites of our conscience in the awareness of being human and of believing in a common destiny.

Pablo Neruda

SEPARATING PAST AND PRESENT

I will not make my relationship with you the container of all my painful history. When I have a powerful overreaction to something that you do, is it you I am reacting to or some deep hurt from my past that has never fully healed? When I allow resentment, anger and mistrust that have their origins outside of our relationship to overwhelm our present together, I neither heal my past nor do I allow us to have our own separate partnership. When I experience feelings in reaction to you that seem to be stronger than appropriate to the situation, I will ask myself what I am really reacting to. Is it something you have done that bothers me or has something you have done triggered unhealed pain from my past? I will make every effort to separate you and us from my own personal history.

Only in relationships can you know yourself, not in
abstraction and certainly not in isolation. The movement of
behavior is the sure guide to yourself, it's the mirror of your
consciousness; this mirror will reveal its content,
the images, the attachments, the fears, the loneliness,
the joy and sorrow. Poverty lies in running away from this,
either in its sublimations or its identities.

J. Krishnamurti

STAYING IN THE GAME

I don't need to be best anymore, or first, or perfect. I find that I am less driven to do that which will make me succeed and more apt to do that which will make me happy. I don't rely on who I think I should be as much as on who I am, and who I am doesn't need to be better than someone else in order to be good enough. I just want to stay in the game, just be a player. I am happy we are together. We do not need to be perfect or even close to it. What's perfection anyway but an idea of the ideal separate from the experience of reality. Ideas are not what ground me, experience is. To open myself up to be with the moment makes available all that I need in order to sustain myself and be happy.

Often people attempt to live their lives backwards;
they try to have more things, or more money, in order to
do more of what they want, so they will be happier.
The way it actually works is the reverse. You must first
be who you really are, then do what you need to
do in order to have what you want.

Margaret Young

Portrait of a Girl   *Edgard Maxence (Nantes, 1871-1954)*

A QUIET PLACE

You live
In a quiet place
Inside my heart.
I find you there
When I least expect you.
You sit in the rooms
Inside my unconscious.
You swim in a river
Inside my soul.
I turn a corner
And I see you there.

I expect you.
I wait for you
Even when I try not to.
I hold you in
the silent memories
that I keep in a basket
beside my bed.
You live there
With me.
We are together
in all those places.

RITUAL

I will respect ritual in our life together. There are daily rituals beginning in the morning. Evening rituals — things we do apart or together that we count on to anchor ourselves. There are events that we share that draw on our humanness and create a bond, a sense of belonging to a community. Rituals appear as habit, but for us they are not empty. Rather they deepen our sense of self and connectedness. Some rituals are sacred and bring us into an experience of God. They are consciousness changing. Others may just assist with transitions in our day. The rituals that we share are important. They act as a catalyst into shared space and experience. They center us and, having done that, set our minds free to explore. They have a quiet level of grandeur all their own. Ritual serves as a gateway into a deeper experience of the self, a more profound level of connectedness. When we engage fully in rituals, we are calling out to the infinite and to our very souls.

Painting is only a bridge linking the painter's mind
with that of the viewer.

Eugene Delacroix

APOLOGY

I will not be afraid to say, "I am sorry." Entrenching myself in a position and refusing to move is not an enlightened way in which to live in relationship. Relationships are give and take, compromise and understanding. Clenching my jaw and setting my chin are not taking care of myself or the relationship. Rather it is a subtle form of self-abuse and blindness to another person. Taking care of myself is much more demanding than that. It requires full honesty, vulnerability and self-disclosure. It asks me to take responsibility for my real thoughts, actions and motives. When I take care of myself by denying and ignoring your feelings, I am creating sickness, hurt and mistrust. Unhealthy positions are black and white, overly understanding and solicitous or rigid and distant. Health is somewhere in between. Our relationship happens in the space between us. It is our common goal, our shared purpose, our commitment and our good will. It is an entity that we create.

There are two ways of spreading light;
To be the candle or the mirror that reflects it.

Edith Wharton

45

GROWING TOGETHER

The part of me that chose you is deeper than I know. The depths of my unconscious reached out to yours. At some unspoken level I chose you to assist me in the continuous process of my own soul-making. Parts of me that come to you may be outside of my immediate vision. The unrequited yearnings, the unfinished childhood, the hidden dreams, all reached out to you for completion and illumination. Being with you is an attempt to see myself — to be with those parts of me that are pulled on by you. If I am wise, I will use our relationship as an opportunity to grow. Growth is messy and painful — it can be confusing and make me doubt myself and you, but growing through my difficult feelings has its own reward in experiencing my expanded self, what I have to take to my life and to all of my relationships. You were not an accidental choice — at a profound level I knew what I was doing and I chose not only someone with whom I liked to be, but someone in whose presence I saw myself, someone with whom I felt I could grow.

Like everybody who is not in love, he imagined
that one chose the person whom one loved after endless
deliberations and on the strength of various
qualities and advantages.

Marcel Proust

Landscape   *Caryuelle d'Aligny*

CHOOSING

I choose you. I choose you with my mind, my soul, my heart and my body. I come to you with all the fear and vulnerability of one who loves and hopes to be loved in return. I allow you to see me quite unadorned, very raw, very pure. I choose you to be my partner in life, to work through petty annoyances, deep sorrow and monumental love. You are the person with whom I have cast my fate, who will influence me in a thousand invisible ways, day after day. We are building selves together, struggling to be more of who we are, comrades in laughter, adversaries in pain. At war, at peace, or on a quiet afternoon, I choose you. We make our home together; we are family, a safe harbor from which to sail and return.

The spring with its leaves and flowers has come into my body . . .

A sweet fountain springs up from the heart of my heart.

And are those your songs that are echoing in the dark caves of my being?

Who but you can hear the hum of the crowded hours that sounds in my
veins today, the glad steps that dance in my breast, the clamour of the
restless life beating its wings in my body?

Rabindranath Tagore

PROJECTING MY NEEDS

*B*ecause I identify with you so strongly and feel a deep conviction, you draw needs, longings, fears and pain from my unconscious. Because these feelings are too painful for me to feel, I project them onto those close to me. It is the way that my unconscious tries to see its contents. I need to recognize that these are really my own feelings, rather than yours, that I am seeing. Once I own them as my own, I can do something about them. The very act of seeing that they are about myself, rather than you, is perhaps the biggest step in healing. It is easy for me to own my good feelings because it doesn't hurt to feel them. The ones that hurt I project outwards in an attempt to get rid of them. Unfortunately when I am not aware that they are my own, I genuinely see them as being about someone else. I get caught up in convincing another person that what I feel is true for them is true for them and I miss the opportunity to better understand myself.

> Should I, after tea and cake and ices,
> Have the strength to force the moment to its crisis?
>
> T. S. Eliot

IDENTIFYING MY OWN NEEDS

The idea of identifying my own needs is to know myself better. This is a deep and painstaking process. Understanding at some basic level what my needs are and being willing to know and feel them is very liberating. It forces me to see what I am like. Filling them is much easier than knowing them. When I focus on filling them rather than knowing them, I run the risk of emotionally blackmailing people close to me because every time I think I have a need, rather than tolerating the experience of sitting with it and feeling it, I ask someone else to fill it for me. This keeps me tied up in an interaction of asking — waiting — getting or asking — waiting — being disappointed. It keeps me in the "superficial supply and demand" dynamic. Knowing my needs does not mean that other people necessarily have to fill them. Knowing them can be information for me.

O young artist, you search for a subject — everything
   is your subject.
Your subject is yourself, your impressions, your
   emotions in the presence of nature.

Eugene Delacroix

HOLDING A PLACE

I will hold a space
for you in which to be:
My gift to you.
A place
in the world
beside me.
I will honor that space
and protect it
and if you hold
a place for me
I will accept and value it.
We two
can do one another
a great service
here
on earth
while we are alive.
We can give
one another
shelter.
We cannot change the wind
or the rain or devastation
of storms.
We cannot make what will
happen
not happen
but we can provide
a feeling of safety
in each other's
arms.

Morning   *Aloys Wach (Munich, 1918)*

SEXUALITY

I will bring my full sexual self to our bed and ask you to do the same. It is not your job to make me sexual nor vice versa. My sensuality is my own; my openness, receptivity and willingness to experiment and be free with you are qualities that I find inside of myself, then talk about and agree upon with you. For me to come to you and wait to be turned on and led through a sexual experience by you is missing the point. We are in this together and we both need to do our part. Our sexual life is deeply bonding and profoundly intimate. It is not about how we perform for each other, but how sensitive, clear and open we are willing to be with one another. What I can have with you is not easily replaced because sex is not only about sex but about love and intimacy. It is a moment when our spiritual and animal selves can be freely expressed and enjoyed. It connects us to each other and to our selves.

Sex and beauty are inseparable, like life
and consciousness. And the intelligence which goes
with sex and beauty, and arises out of sex
and beauty, is intuition.

D. H. Lawrence

FLEXIBILITY

I have been loyal to a search for selfhood but in my finding and standing by myself I will not forget that you exist also. I will not use my personal quest as an excuse to shut you out or take care of myself at your expense. That would only be replicating dysfunction or putting a new face on abuse. If I push you away in order to protect myself without taking your feelings into consideration, I am creating a wound in you and in our relationship. By my behavior, I am causing a rupture from which we will have to heal at some later time. My goal in life is self-reliance, not a life of emotional isolation. If I am not willing mentally and emotionally to reverse roles with you and see things from your eyes also, how can I ever really understand you? If I become rigid in my point of view because I think it is healthier, the rigidity itself denotes a lack of health. Balance involves more than one object. Understanding requires flexibility.

We thought we were done with these things but we were wrong.

We thought, because we had power, we had wisdom.

Stephen Vincent Benet

STRETCHING BEYOND

I will stretch beyond what I perceive to be my limits with you. When I feel that I have given enough, understood enough and still feel stuck, I will not run from this place. I will feel this "stuckness" fully, observe it and let it have its day. By letting myself stay with it rather than walking away, I give myself the opportunity to experience the feeling. It will change — it will transform — it will break apart into many separate little emotional images, all of which will provide me with more information about myself, on my own and in relationship with you. Inner windows will open up and I shall see further into the variables that created the emotional traffic jam in me and in our relationship. Next time I feel as if there is no way out or around, I'll wait a little while, relax and allow things to change. I don't need to force my way through and control the outcome. What is the outcome anyway — why does it have to be the way I picture it? Why should I limit it?

There is no remedy for love but to love more.

Henry David Thoreau

HIDING

Our relationship is not a place to hide, either from myself or the rest of the world. If I use it for this purpose, it will shrink in size and in its ability to nurture me. I will start to expect what it cannot give me and drain it of its energy. I need to engage fully in life on my own two legs. This relationship should not be a crutch to hold me up. I can lean on you in times of need as you can on me, but neither of us will benefit from carrying one another. Our love is not a place to hide from ourselves. If we use it this way, we will look for ourselves in one another and we will be disappointed when we do not find ourselves there. We can only find ourselves within. We can offer each other refuge and support in times of need, but hiding will create darkness and darkness can lead to blindness. We are here to help each other see.

Take love when it is given,
But never think to find it
A sure escape from sorrow
Or a complete repose.

Sara Teasdale

REAL VALUE

I will value what I have. In this world of object worship, it is so easy to forget that the only true wealth is inner wealth and what we share with one another. Life is relationship. I do not wish to lose you in order to understand your importance in my life. I will treat us well and respect the meaning of your presence. Just by being in this committed, loving relationship with me, you are a powerful source of support. We are thousands of things to one another. I look around and see a society that overvalues objects and undervalues people. At the end of the day I cannot hold hands with a bank account, success or even a profession. I cannot reach out and touch these things in the night. The objects of this world serve me only when I can keep them in perspective. When I cannot, they rule me. I will remember today what is really important — what truly matters.

Love is the only gold.
Alfred Lord Tennyson

A HOLDING ENVIRONMENT

Today I will bear witness to my own thoughts and feelings. I will create a quiet "holding environment" within myself where my essence can be contained in safety and support. If I expect you to be my holding environment, I will be at loose ends when you are not present. You have enough to handle being present for yourself on a consistent basis. How can you do for me what you can only just do for yourself? I will hold myself. At times I can look to you to help me when I cannot help myself — but only at times. If it becomes my way of life, neither of us will be able to sustain it. I have quiet within, I have a heart and a spirit and a mind. All of these parts of me can work together to make serene inner space where I can be held in safety and comfort.

Affirmation of life is the spiritual act
by which man ceases to live unreflectively and
begins to devote himself to his life with reverence
in order to raise it to its true value. To affirm
life is to deepen, to make more inward
and to exalt the will to live.

Albert Schweitzer

Amie de Plomb   *Theodore Rousseau (Paris, 1812-1867)*

Landscape with Boat   *Jean-Baptiste-Camille Corot (Paris, 1796-1875)*

BEING ALONE

I am ultimately alone in life. When I can learn to tolerate, even embrace my feelings of aloneness, I am then able to be with someone else without substituting myself for them or them for me. The void that I fear falling into is just more of me. I will grow stronger if I can learn to abide my feelings of aloneness. This is different from being alone. Feeling alone can happen in a crowd, in the marketplace or in the center of my family or friends. When it happens, rather than ask another to fill me up, I will sit with, experience and make friends with it, knowing that it is only when I can be alone that I can then share myself with another.

> *Only in solitude do we find ourselves;*
> *and in finding ourselves, we find in ourselves*
> *all our brothers in solitude.*
>
> Miguel De Unamuro

PUSHING YOU AWAY

I can push you away when I need to. I worry so about being pushed away by you that I play the victim and cast you in the role of the aggressor. I am not just a reactor; I am also proactive. When I need space, I can have it. I have a right to some room to breathe if I feel cramped or hurt or misunderstood. I can stand on my own for a few hours without my life falling apart. I can say, "I need a break." When I am not able to decide to give myself the room I need to process my uncomfortable, upsetting feelings, I may create a crisis in order to get away. I do not need your approval to have a little quiet time. Nor do I need your permission or blessing. You may not even need to know what I am doing. But I will know. I am giving myself room to feel.

You gain strength, courage and confidence
by every experience in which you really stop to
look fear in the face. You are able to say to yourself,
"I lived through this horror. I can take the next
thing that comes along." . . . You must do
the thing you think you cannot do.

Anna Eleanor Roosevelt

REFLECTIONS AND SECRETS

*Y*our actions are not necessarily a reflection on me, nor mine a reflection on you. In partnership I forget that people are capable of telling us apart. Though we may reflect each other, we are different people. It is an important distinction to keep in mind. When I see each thing that you do in your life as saying something about me, I become a frantic monitor of your every action. If you have an activity I do not like, it is your activity, not mine. If you act in a way that is inappropriate, you are embarrassing yourself. Though I may also feel embarrassed, I need to remember that I am not you and you are not me. Even when other people confuse us for each other, it is important that I keep our identities straight. If I do not, I will be living for two, thinking for two and reacting for two. It is hard enough to do these things for myself without the added complication that arises when I weave you into me.

There are no secrets better kept than
the secrets everybody guesses.

George Bernard Shaw

FALLING INTO NEGATIVITY

I am determined to have all I can have in my relationship today. Negativity is all around and the temptation to fall into it is sometimes more than I can resist. Living up to negative ideals is sometimes easier than living up to positive ones. Conducting myself with care and wisdom requires a sort of discipline that I am not always able to come up with. It is not easy to make room for my real feelings without allowing them to run away with me in destructive ways. Thinking that I must surpass what I grew up with or feeling inferior to it are traps that I can fall into. It takes courage and creativity to tailor our relationship to us. Some days accepting myself as I am, you as you are, can seem almost too difficult. It requires that I sit with my own pain and fear rather than project them onto you in the form of inhuman expectations or undeserved anger.

pro jec'tion:

4. in psychiatry, the unconscious act or process of ascribing to others one's own ideas or impulses, especially when such ideas or impulses are considered undesirable.

Webster's Dictionary

FAITH

I will have faith in our relationship. When you feel far away from me, I will have faith that you will return, stronger, newer, with more of you. When I feel that you are disappearing under the weight of change, day-to-day living and your own search, I will know that you are still there even though I cannot see you. When my heart wanders and looks for what it feels it cannot find with you, I will remind myself that my heart is big enough to include more than just you or just me and that you need not be all things I want to be enough. And when you go to others to find what you cannot find with me, I will remember that I cannot be all to you — that your having other sources of sustenance is natural and good and does not in any way reduce your love for me.

Faith must trample under foot all reason,
sense and understanding.

Martin Luther

HEALING

I believe in healing. The wounds that we may have caused each other can heal if we allow them to. When they begin to heal, I will not keep picking and pounding at them, making them hurt all over again. Just as a body needs rest and quiet to heal so does our relationship. I will create optimum conditions of calm, support and love so that we can feel safe and well again. Anybody can get sick for a while. Any relationship can too. Just as I would not turn in my body, I will not turn in my relationship. It just needs a little R&R until it is back to normal. If we need help we can ask for it. Why should we be any different than anything else in this world? I will take care of what I have, remembering that it is as subject to disruption from the environment as any other living thing.

The strongest of all warriors are these two —
time and patience

Leo Tolstoy

Head of a Female Saint   *Anonymous, French Romantic School*

Flower

Anonymous (c. 1820)

A QUIET KIND OF LOVE

Ours is a quiet kind of love.
We two know one another.
Your unconscious
   movements
Are etched into my
   unconscious.
The sound of your voice
Lives within my inner
   hearing.
Your touch is a part of me.
I feel it when you are not
   there.

I know it in my very depths.
I take your heart into my
   hands.
Your life into my life.
Your soul into my soul.
You live at my very center
And yet we are two —
Very separate —
Closer than close.
Both are meant to be.

CO-OBSESSION

You and I will go through many periods of change in our lives. It will be enough for me to handle my own changing without becoming tied up in yours. When you become obsessed by something, it is time for me to back up and give you and myself more space. If, instead, I see your obsession as a time for me to move in close, I will become wrapped up in an obsession that has its roots in another person's psyche. I will not have the benefit of playing something out within myself that needs to be seen — I will just drive myself and you crazy with my obsession about your obsession. Obsession with anything is not healthy or balanced. I experience losing you in your preoccupation, just as you are losing yourself to it. Then I try to find you by getting involved. Soon we are both out of balance. Next time when you are obsessed with something, I will stay centered. That way, at least one of us will be locatable.

Why destroy your present happiness by
a distant misery which may never come at all?
For every substantial grief has twenty shadows and most
of the shadows are of your own making.

Sydney Smith

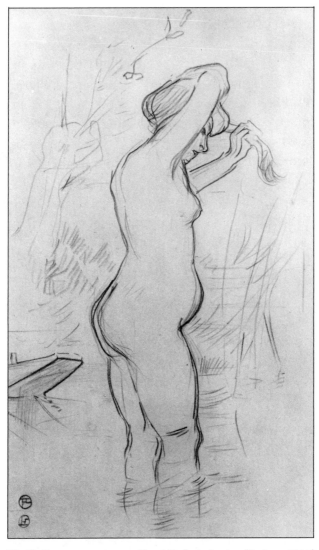

The Bather   *Henri Toulouse-Lautrec (Paris, c. 1894)*

MYTHS

ften I hold an image of a relationship in my mind that is an impossible dream disembodied from real life, unattainable and unreal. When I ask our relationship to conform to something that is not possible and cannot be sustained in day-to-day life, the discrepancy between who we are and who I think we should be divides us from ourselves. When we are divided from ourselves, we have less that is real to bring to each other. We get depressed and discouraged about what we are not and disconnected from all that we are. When I ask us to be in good form all the time, I ask too much. I insist on the impossible and I use, as my measuring stick, relationships that are not even real. They are a construction of someone's ideas about people who in reality do not exist. I will examine the parts of our relationship that I hold hostage to my fantasies of how a relationship "should" be. There is no crime in just having the relationship that we have; we don't need to follow a prescribed pattern to be all right.

The great enemy of truth is very often not a lie,
deliberate, contrived and dishonest. But the myth,
persistent, persuasive and unrealistic.

John Fitzgerald Kennedy

ALL THAT I FEEL ABOUT YOU

Unless I accept you as you are, I will not know how to live around you. If I don't look clearly at your difficult sides, I will not protect myself from them. If I don't credit your strengths, I will not be able to benefit from them. When my energy goes into changing you rather than accepting you, I enter into a lifelong obsession in which I rarely succeed in altering you but I do succeed in losing myself in the trying. Trying to change you is a vain attempt and I am the biggest loser. I not only devote my time and creative energy to remaking you in a different image, but I try to remake myself and our relationship as well. I need to give myself space to feel all of my feelings about you. I don't like it when I don't like certain things about you. I find it threatening, and so in order not to have to sit with those uncomfortable feelings, I imagine changing you into something different, much like a child would fantasize turning a mean parent into a nice one. I will do better in the long run if I can face all of my feelings about you, good and bad.

Peace of mind comes from not wanting to change others,
but by simply accepting them as they are.
True acceptance is always without
demands and expectations.

Gerald G. Jampolsky

RELEASING THE PAST

I will attempt to allow the past to be the past. So often when we argue, each of us dredges up painful material from the past to illustrate and reillustrate our points. Some of what we go over doesn't even apply anymore. At times what we bring up has long since been worked through but neither of us can resist the opening to drag it out again. It is one thing to bring something forward because it needs to be healed and quite another to recreate pain and drama over and over again due to a morbid attachment. Just for today I will leave well enough alone and see how that works. I will assume that our relationship can work out and not burden it with excess baggage from past circumstances. Just for today I will be kind to myself and let that kindness take the form of keeping myself out of unnecessary trouble. Just for today I will know that my serenity comes first and I will let dissension go.

Let us not burden our remembrance with
a heaviness that's gone.

Shakespeare

REGRET

If I have done something truly hurtful to you, I will not run away from the pain and guilt I feel. Feeling those feelings is really the only way to clean them out of my system. When I will not allow myself to experience my regret fully, I set up a cycle in which I have to hurt you or someone else or myself as a way of getting rid of the feeling when it arises within me. I will also allow you the space to feel your own regret when you behave unkindly toward me. Often when you hurt me I react with anger and I hide my hurt feelings from you. When that is all I let you see of me, I give us my anger to focus on and we both get lost in it. I don't get the understanding and comfort I need from you and I give you fuel for focusing on my behavior rather than your own. I will stay with my real feelings when you hurt me so that you will have time and space to see the error of your own ways.

Whenever you start measuring somebody, measure
him right, child, measure him right. Make sure you have
taken into account what hills and valleys he came
through before he got to wherever he is.

Lorraine Hansberry

REJECTION

*B*ecause, at times, I feel rejected by you does not mean that I have to reject myself. You may be rejecting me for reasons that have nothing to do with me. Perhaps you felt rejected by a parent and get frightened when you get too close to another person. Maybe you don't feel good about yourself and you act out that painful feeling by rejecting me. Whatever it is, I need not always take it personally. When I reject myself because I feel rejected by you, I lose myself and only deepen a painful dynamic. I become filled with self doubt and insecurity. I hold myself responsible for things I have nothing to do with and I give up all of my serenity to your changing moods. There is a way for me not to allow you to hold the scorecard in your hand when it comes to my own self-acceptance. I will create a space in which I hold myself safe, secure and unconditionally loved.

Oh seek, my love, your newer way
I'll not be left in sorrow
So long as I have yesterday
Go take your damned tomorrow!

Dorothy Parker

UNDERSTANDING CONFLICT

I do not need to give myself away in my relationship with you. My conditioning has taught me that the best way to avoid conflict is to fuse my identity and desire with another person. Over time I become resentful for having put my wants aside, and I long for the person I used to be, the one I have chosen to ignore. Today I understand that a good relationship is not without conflict. Conflict is natural throughout the course of a day. A close relationship will inevitably include plenty.

Each of us needs our own life. I cannot live yours and you cannot live mine — it doesn't work that way. When we try, each of us experiences a loss of identity and connection with the self. Our connection with the rest of the world is through the self. Through our personal soul we access a universal consciousness and the soul force or consciousness of another person. In order to do this I have to live in my own skin and allow you to live in yours. Though, on the surface, this may decrease our connection, on a deeper level it increases it. Through our highly developed selves or souls we can truly have our most meaningful and satisfying sense of relatedness.

*I will work in my own way, according to
the light that is in me.*

Lydia Maria Child

Untitled   *Leo Gausson (c. 1886)*

ENJOYMENT

I will allow you to have fun — fun that has nothing to do with me, knowing that the positive energy you receive will eventually be shared with me in one form or another. I will let myself have enjoyment and meaningful connections with people in my own life. The experience that I collect in a life separate from you will enhance what we have together. If we are really connected, then being separate need not threaten us. The connection we make is through acceptance and understanding, mutual respect and a sense of place and belonging. The fun you have apart from me need not diminish what we have together. Rather it should enhance it. When we fill our cups from all that life has to offer, we are less demanding of one another. I can trust that my enjoyment apart from you and yours apart from me does not divide us. I can better allow us both the space to engage more fully in our own lives, knowing that it needn't mean that we will not be there for one another. There is more to life than each other, but your presence in my life makes all the rest feel sweeter.

Most people ask for happiness on condition.
Happiness can only be felt if you
don't set any condition.

Arthur Rubinstein

HOPE

*I*t is all right for me to have hope for our relationship and to harbor that hope deep inside of me in the silence of my heart. There will be times when I cannot share it with you. Times when each of us may be too distracted by life or our changing insides to even remember what it means to be in a partnership. Long periods when I am not getting what I need from you in order to feel secure. This does not mean that I have to give up hope or that it is foolish to hope. It is only foolish when it keeps me from allowing myself to feel what I really feel. Hope is something that I have a right to — no matter what. It is also something that I can feel and then let go of so that I do not cling to it and maintain myself in that state. Anxious wishing and attempting "to hold on until" will only keep me locked into a cycle of hope and despair. There is another kind of hope that just abides because somehow it has confidence in the ever-present beauty of life.

"Hope" is the thing with feathers —
That perches in the soul —
And sings the tune without the words —
And never stops — at all.

Emily Dickinson

RETRIBUTION

Today I see the great temptation when my partner behaves in hurtful insensitive ways, to behave that way myself, in return. I realize that in getting even with another person, I am getting even with myself; I lose my own serenity and any possibility of changing the interaction for the better is lost. If someone is acting in ways that are hurtful, it is because they are in a bad place themselves. When I behave in kind, I am joining them. I am clearheaded enough to realize that the way in which they're acting is undesirable, and I need not do the same myself.

And though I have the gift of prophecy and understand all mysteries, and all knowledge; and though I have all faith, so that I could remove mountains, and have not love, I am nothing.

Love suffereth long, and is kind; love envieth not, love vaunteth not itself, is not puffed up.

Love never faileth: but where there be prophesies, they shall fail; whether there be tongues, they shall cease; whether there be knowledge, it shall vanish away.

I Corinthians 13

PERFECTIONISM

I will not ask each day of our relationship to be the perfect cameo of health and bliss. If I do that, I will be asking us both to live a lie because life doesn't work that way. Relationships are tied to reality and subject to those forces. Allowing them to ride the waves of life will give them more fortitude and flexibility than trying to get them to be better than life. Beauty is in the eyes of the beholder. I will attempt to see beauty in things as they are, rather than things as I feel they should be. When I hold us to my image of how we should be before I allow myself to feel secure, I sentence myself to a state of frequent insecurity. Nothing is exactly as I want it to be. That is not the nature of life. If I could learn to feel contentment with things as they are instead of always trying to get them to conform to my ideals, I would probably be much better off.

Would that life were like the shadow cast by a wall or a tree,
but it is like the shadow of a bird in flight.

The Talmud

A Flock of Sheep in Summer Pastures

Charles Francois Daubigny
(Paris, 1817-1878)

BEING

I do not strive toward perfection with you
But see perfection in what already is.
Beauty is in the eyes of the beholder.
If I know how to see beauty,
   it will surround me forever.
If my world has to prove itself to me in order for me
   to love it,
I number my happy days.
There is no reason that you or I have to be perfect.
Accepting perfection in things as they are
   gives them a kind of space to be beautiful.
Wonder and beauty are not locked in what is
But in my ability to recognize them
Wherever they may be.

CHANGING DYNAMICS

I will be open today to the shifting moods of our relationship with each other and with those around us. Dynamics are always changing, all is always in a state of flux. If I do not like the way that I am perceived by others or the way that I look at them, I will be open to change. My very act of being open creates favorable conditions for movement to take place. The waters beneath interpersonal dynamics are constantly flowing in all directions. When I see them as fixed, I keep myself in static relationships wherein the feelings lack spontaneity and what takes place has a strange sense of dislocation from the rest of my life, both inner and outer. When I am willing to allow the moment to have its voice — to do its work — life takes on a new sense of buoyancy and enjoyment. Situations that used to perplex me seem to work themselves out naturally.

The opinions which we hold of one another,
our relations with friends and kinfolk are in no sense
permanent, save in appearance, but are extremely
fluid as the sea itself.

Marcel Proust

SPIRITUALITY IN RELATIONSHIPS

I will learn to see a Higher Power within you, within me and at work in our relationship. Our relationship has an alive and spiritual feeling to it. It is an arena in which I can experience divine expression if I choose to use it as such. It can help me to grow — to learn to be a more tolerant and loving person. It is an opportunity to see who I really am in relation to another person. Our relationship can give me perspective on myself as I see myself reflected through another person's eyes, while learning to balance that outer reflection with my inner one. It can teach me patience and show me that I cannot control another person, while still maintaining a sense of newness, wonder and spontaneity. My relationship can help me to learn to connect with more than just you or me — it can be a door to other places.

There are very few human beings who receive
the truth, complete and staggering, by instant illumination.
Most of them acquire it fragment by fragment, on a
small scale, by successive developments,
cellularly, like a laborious mosaic.

Anais Nin

DIFFERENT PATHS

Today I release you from all false contracts — quiet little ways in which I hold you hostage to my own needs and fantasies — whether or not they concur with your own. What am I doing trying to recreate you in my image of who and what you should be? You have a right to your own particular variety of fulfillment and enjoyment. If I try to get you to live life as I feel you should live it, I will drain away your spirit. Then, after it has disappeared by inches, I will long for the person I fell in love with. When your ways of doing things threaten me, I will remind myself that that is part of being close to another person. You have the right to be you. If we can each remain ourselves, we will have more to bring to one another than if we have reorganized our personalities to fit the job description of the other.

The first thing to learn in intercourse with
others is noninterference with their own peculiar ways
of being happy, provided those ways do not assume
to interfere by violence with ours.

William James

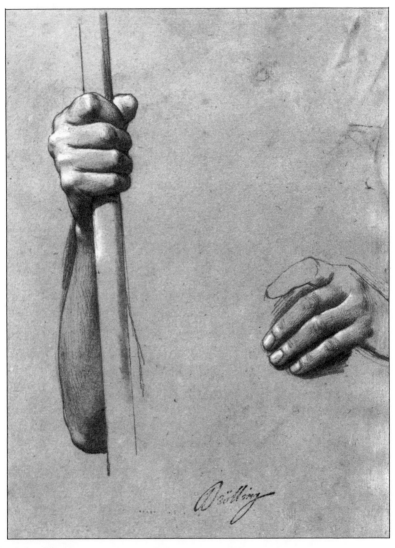

Study of Hands   *Martin Drolling, (Paris 1752-1817)*

UNFINISHED BUSINESS

All that remains unfinished within me seeks to play itself out in the intimate arena of our relationship. The open tensions and unfelt or unexpressed pain of past situations that never came to a comfortable closure will be activated by the closeness that we experience together. When we love one another, the experience of that love is like light in a dark room. It illuminates what heretofore lay in the shadows of the unconscious. The light that it sheds can be harsh and painful because it awakens sleeping monsters. When the monsters wake up, they rise to their full and terrifying size, frightening us both and making us think the other is responsible for them. In truth these are the forgotten elements of our own souls coming to us to see, feel and release. I will remember this when I need it.

For my part I believe in the forgiveness of
sin and the redemption of ignorance.

Adlai Stevenson

TELLING ALL

I will learn when to keep my mouth closed. It's very tempting for me to say all — to tell you each hurt, each bit of anger or mistrust. But there's a difference between opening my heart to you and opening my mouth. When I open my heart, I have two-way vision and I can empathize with both of our positions. When my words come only from my mouth without being first felt and considered, they feel different to both of us. Our conversations become less of a sharing and more of a debate. You do not need to know everything that goes through my mind. Living with another person will always have irritating features. We will rub up against one another in ways that annoy us both; it's to be expected. Whether or not we bother one another is not a sign of our rightness as a couple — only part and parcel of being two grown adults trying to integrate complicated lives, personalities, property, family and so on. A certain amount of discomfort is natural and needn't be worked out — only accepted.

Thinking is an experiment dealing with
small quantities of energy, just as a general moves
miniature figures over a map before
setting his troops in action.

Sigmund Freud

THE BOTTOM LINE

I am a part of a stream of life. My choice of you as a partner was greatly influenced by my past, how I grew up, who was important to me, the nature of my relationship with my parents and a thousand other factors that went into building my psyche. In this sense my past is continued through my union with you. We pass ourselves on through any progeny we may bear or through those lives that we touch. You live within me much in the way my parents or siblings do, at a deep and indelible level. You are part of my sense of continuity in my life — this is the way it is passed on — through those you love and touch and shape your lives and spirits with. Leaving you would be leaving that part of myself. It can be done but there would be a price to pay. A good negotiator always makes sure that the gain is greater than the loss. A good negotiator looks at the bottom line.

Life is a series of collisions with the future;
it is not a sum of what we have been
but what we yearn to be.

Jose Ortega y Gasset

MY OWN LIFE

I need to make meaningful, nurturing connections all around me. Sometimes I push nurturing away; if it feels too good, it frightens me. In an effort to feel safe I hold on too tightly to your presence. Because I know you as a fixture in my life, I feel safe doing this but I am learning that this safety is an illusion. It actually diminishes my ability to take in nurturing experiences. When I limit the source to just you, I deny the possibility of other things happening. I become pessimistic in my outlook on life if I reduce my scope of vision to the few objects and people closest to me. I hem myself in without knowing it. My overdependency on you actually lessens my feeling of safety. I will seek to anchor myself within both psychically and spiritually.

*Each time you accept a thought that is greater
than what you have accepted as your standard, that thought
activates yet another part of your brain into purposeful use. Each time
you do that, the greater thought will offer itself as a carrier
to expand your reasoning from that point. That will activate
other portions of your brain for more thought, for more receiving,
for more knowing. You know, it is very simple to be a genius.
All you have to do is think for yourself.*

Ramtha

La Rue   *Theophile-Alexandre Steinlen (Lausanne 1859-Paris 1901)*

PERSPECTIVE

While I believe, as Plato said, "The life which is unexamined is not worth living," I will not confuse self-examination with excessive scrutiny. Looking too closely can produce the same lack of understanding and perspective as not looking enough. If I want to view a painting, I move back so that I can see all of it. If I am too close, I miss the full picture. If I am too far, I can't see the forms or colors clearly. The best seats in a theater are a little back from the stage. The front row puts me so near to the play that I get lost in the actor's torn sleeve or his perspiration. The back row makes me miss too much of the action and sound. So it is with my relationship. When I look too closely, detail takes on too much meaning, focus and attention. When I don't look closely enough, I disengage from what is really going on. I will look for the right distance from which to examine my relationship with you.

If I had a formula for bypassing trouble,
I would not pass it round. Trouble creates a capacity to
handle it. I don't embrace trouble; that's as bad as treating
it as any enemy. But I do say meet it as a friend, for you'll see a lot
of it and had better be on speaking terms with it.

Oliver Wendell Holmes

JEALOUSY

I will look at myself closely when I feel jealous of you. Why should I keep you from your own happiness and personal satisfaction because it threatens me? Being jealous is not good for our relationship and it is not good for me as a person. I can use our relationship as a place to grow. When I feel myself getting tied up in all of my worst fantasies, I will step back and examine what I can change within me to allow myself to move away from a painful, destructive position. Though I may have things about which to be jealous, will it really benefit me to indulge myself in that feeling? It is a beautiful thing to be able to feel joy in another person's happiness. Not only does it expand me as a spiritual person, but it gives me more moments of pleasure in my own life and connects me with others in a positive light.

Beware of envy: For to grudge any man
an advantage in person and fortune is to censure
the liberality of providence, and be angry
at the goodness of God.

Shelley

PERSONAL GROWTH

When I get lost in the struggles of our relationship, I forget that ultimately the reason for me to seek the most positive, constructive path is to liberate myself. Our relationship offers me incredible opportunities to grow as a person. If I can see the changes that I make in myself not as something I am doing to please you, but as changes I make in order to become a fuller, more expressive, empathic person, I will be keeping the locus of control where it belongs, within me. A relationship is a wonderful opportunity to expand one's understanding of self. It acts as a mirror for our deepest patterns of behavior and brings to the surface unconscious material to be worked out in the present. I will use this relationship as an arena in which to grow myself.

It takes two to see one.

C. S. Lewis

FRIENDSHIP

*Y*ou are my friend, an amiable presence in my life, someone with whom I can pass time in comfort. We make plans together that sound appealing. We chat. We listen to one another and spill out our innermost thoughts. We share the shallow, the first impressions, the nonsense. I am so used to you that I hardly know the thousand tiny ways in which I know you. I understand you not with my thoughts but with my being. I would have a hard time describing you to someone because so much of you has integrated into me. Though we are two, we are connected at a level that is indescribably deep. I have passed countless hours in your presence and heard as many of your words spoken as any one person has. I have seen you in endless situations, observed how you break your bread, how you sip your tea, how you stroll along a garden path. Your movements, your voice, your touch are all drawn into my memory like paintings on a wall. They span time, they span my life as I know it. You are a part of me in so many ways, so very many ways.

Do not use a hatchet to remove a fly from
your friend's forehead.

Chinese Proverb

OVER AND OVER

Over and over again in a silent corner of my heart
I observe your presence within me —
You have traced your image
Across the landscape of my life and etched your being
   into my psyche
You are a part of me in ways I hardly understand
And still forever a stranger —
A person apart
While at the same moment living within my inner
   vision
You are a thousand times me and a million times
   yourself
So frightening in your power to hurt me
So endearing in your love that makes all the rest
Disappear at your touch
Or the sound of your footsteps.

DISTANCE

I will let there be distance in our relationship. Without distance neither of us can take in a full breath of ourselves. An appropriate distance gives each of us room to be our own person, pursue our own interests and follow our own uniqueness. In this way, when we come together, we bring ourselves, not only our version of the other's expectations and our own. Too much distance creates loneliness and isolation, but too little can have a similar effect. In each other's presence, we become lonely for ourselves and the people we used to be. Then, as a reaction, we need too much distance to find ourselves again. There is space enough in our relationship for each of us to be.

A good marriage is that in which each appoints
the other guardian of his solitude. Once the realization is
accepted that even between the closest human beings infinite distances
continue to exist, a wonderful living side by side can grow up,
if they succeed in loving the distance between them which
makes it possible for each to see the other
whole and against a wide sky.

Rainer Maria Rilke

PLAYING MY ROLE

I will play my role of being your partner but I will not become the role. I am still entitled to a self and an individual life even though I am in full partnership with you. If I lose myself to the role, eventually I will be relating to you one step removed from my real nature. A role, by definition, is something I take on and off. Though I am committed to you completely, I can still step out of the role of your partner and into other roles throughout the course of my day. I need this role relief or I will become fatigued and jaded on the subject of us and resent you for taking up too much space in my head. The more I allow myself to play a variety of roles in my life through which I experience nurturing, competence and satisfaction, the less I will demand that you supply all of these things and vice versa.

The Japanese have a word for it.
It's judo — the art of conquering by yielding.
The western equivalent of judo is, "Yes, dear."

J. P. McEvoy

LOVE AND HATE

I will seek a balance in our relationship. If I insist on too much love, it may seek to balance itself out with too much hate. Familiarity breeds contempt. Pushing any feeling beyond its natural course gives rise to its opposite. I will do what comes naturally. Our love is there like a water table beneath the earth. We don't have to prove it over and over again. If I make each little thing a proof of your love, then I risk making each little thing a proof of your contempt. We do not need to be as shallow as that. We can rest in quiet knowing that we are there for one another in the depths of our souls. Gushiness does not mean love, rather it is a compensation for what I unconsciously fear is not there. Excessive attentiveness has its opposite on the flip side. It gives way to a need to run, to ignore and hide. Then overattention returns to compensate. It's a love/hate dynamic and painful at both ends. Love is a quiet thing. It abides; it need not be shown off or overdone. It can just be.

Men stumble over the truth from time to time,
but most men pick themselves up and hurry
off as if nothing happened.

Winston Churchill

The Falls at Terni   *J.J.X. Bidauld (Terni, c. 1800)*

A LONG-TERM RELATIONSHIP

*I*f we are to have a relationship stretched long over time, we will have to allow each other to change. What is appropriate for one stage of life does not necessarily work for another. When we have a family, our attentions go toward building a life, a home, a place to be. Later, we face different challenges. How can we develop a relationship that is secure and trusting yet gives each of us room to pursue our own lives? How can we find a balance between enough togetherness and enough independence? What needs to happen for us to feel sufficiently connected so that we can flow freely in and out of each other's space without losing one another? Where do I begin, you leave off and vice-versa? What do we really need from each other to feel safe, and which expectations are excessive? If we are to last, we need to be flexible and willing to throw out what doesn't work and try new things. We can make experiments and take little risks — we can change and grow.

Marriage is not a finished affair. No matter
to what age you live, love must be continuously consolidated.
Being considerate, thoughtful and respectful without ulterior
motives is the key to a satisfactory marriage.

Pamphlet from
Chinese Family Planning Center

INNER WORK

I am willing to do the inner work that it will take to have a relationship in my life. Every endeavor that is worthwhile takes work. Why should my relationship with you be any different? I will not become arrogant taking you for granted and over-rating myself, nor will I underrate myself and get lost in pleasing you. I will keep in front of my eyes all that we mean to one another and not debilitate our love by harping endlessly on the areas where we are less than ideal. Everyone has problems and disappointments in life. It doesn't mean you stop living. No relationship is perfect, even wanting it to be is its own sort of phobic reaction. When I am afraid of life, I separate it into unrelated sections. I want each section to prove itself to me in order for me to feel secure and worthwhile. Life is meant to be lived hour by hour, day by day. It is not only an act of endurance but also one of surrender.

You have to work constantly at rejuvenating a relationship. You can't just count on its being okay, or it will tend toward a hollow commitment, devoid of passion and intimacy. People need to put the kind of energy into it that they put into their children or career.

Robert Sternberg

LEARNING FROM LIFE

There is much for me to learn from life by quiet observation. When I am patient and open, life unfolds itself and its wisdom to me. When my mind is cluttered with "shoulds" and endless desires, I keep its beauty from entering my heart. There is no need to strain. All that I gain by strain comes with a price tag. I cannot force you to be other than what you choose to be without bending you out of shape. When I force myself to be someone other than I am, my real self comes back to haunt me. A relationship cannot be real if the two people in it are living a lie. What would be so wrong if we came to our relationship as ourselves and learned from one another? Our differences attract us to one another and create diversity and balance, but still we attempt daily to recreate one another in our own image. I like you the way you are. Why should I work so hard to change you? Where you are different from me, you are interesting. Where I don't like it, I don't like it. Big deal. Whoever said we had to be alike to get along?

The man who has become a thinking being feels
a compulsion to give to every will-to-live the same reverence
for life that he gives to his own.

Albert Schweitzer

OUR TAPESTRY

We have woven a tapestry of our life together. Whether or not we are pleased, it is what we have woven. It represents us and what we have put into being us. To me it is beautiful and valuable and precious. I could not give it up without giving up a part of my heart, my soul, who I am. So much of me has been woven into you and so much of you has been woven into me. Pulling the threads apart would tear at me inside. I cannot pretend that my relationship with you is less than it is. Some days I feel as if we live in a world that doesn't understand relationships or really support them. If I am not getting all that I want, the world I live in tells me to get out, to get my needs met, to ask for more. All that is valid, but it is only part of the story. Life is long and, if I am to be with you for the duration, there will be times when my needs aren't met and I'm not getting what I want. Just as my life will not always go smoothly on my own, how can it always go smoothly with you.

Pains do not hold a marriage together.
It is threads, hundreds of tiny threads which sew
people together through the year. That's what makes a
marriage last — more than passion or even sex.

Simone Signoret

GREENER GRASS

I will not be betrayed by the illusion of something better always around the corner. I will learn to work with and value what I have. Anything requires tending. A beautiful garden untended will turn to weeds in three years — so will a beautiful relationship. Anything that I ignore or abuse will only last so long. To cast it aside and start all over again is missing the point. I need to look at myself and what in my own actions has brought something wonderful into a state of disrepair. Even if I have been hurt, the way back to myself is not through hurting back or being tough. If I feel hurt by you, I will get farther if I quietly remove myself and let you sit with your own offensive behavior. Eventually you will see the error of your ways just as I do under the same circumstances and, if we don't, at least we will not escalate into something too ugly to come back from. We can forgive and forget quite a lot, but we can also go too far. I will exercise some caution.

Because a work of art does not aim at reproducing
natural appearances, it is not, therefore, an escape from
life . . . but an expression of a significance of life,
a stimulation to greater effort in living.

Henry Moore

107

JOURNEY INWARDS

Ours is not an exercise
of the mind
but a journey of the soul.
When we mistake the
tasks and trials
of our relationship
for superficialities
we divide ourselves
from a deeper purpose.
You are the perfect
vehicle through which
I can better
vindicate and
experience myself.

A mirror of my
hunger and thirst,
when I chose you,
I chose a path to me.
You are the wind
that pushes at my
shadowy depths,
the siren's song
that draws me to
the edge of the precipice
of my own being.
The immortal mind
that holds my body
in its arms.

Untitled   *Aloys Wach (Munich, c. 1918)*

THE TEMPORARY NATURE OF THINGS

*I*n order to be with you fully, I need to live with the fear of losing you. Life holds no guarantees. If our relationship is alive, anything can happen. Nothing is permanent — though events and circumstances appear stable, they can be turned upside down when I least expect it. There is nothing anyone can do about this. When I accept the temporary nature of life and relationships, two things happen. First, aspects of us that could be troublesome seem less serious because I understand that nothing is forever. Second, I treasure you more because I know that each day with you is a gift. It is important to be in touch with the deeper nature of life to understand the meaning of things. I will give myself the quiet, rest and meditative solitude that I require in order to get in touch with all that lies beneath the surface.

The good life is one inspired by love
and guided by knowledge.
(On second thought, the good life starts only
when you stop wanting a better one.)

Bertrand Russell

OVERFUNCTIONING

I will let go now. I have seen enough of life to understand that expectations, preconceptions and unnecessarily rigid standards do not bring happiness, peace of mind or enjoyment. I can wait till life beats this lesson into my head a thousand times or I can allow myself to learn the lesson through quiet observation of myself and others. What I can let be generally can let me be. When I get overly attached and enmeshed in situations, they have too much impact on me. There is no reason for me to take each little thing so seriously that I lose my serenity. I don't have to be like an idling car, constantly revved up for action. If I am, by the time I need to act, I will be exhausted and ineffective. I will learn when to put my foot on the gas and when to turn my motor off.

But my mother had no dreams to lay on my children.
She had tried . . . and succeeded . . . and failed with my sister
and me. She was done with that now and her grandsons wouldn't
defeat her. Or disappoint her. Or prove anything — anything
good or anything bad — about her. And I saw her free of
ambition, free of the need to control, free of anxiety.
Free — as she liked to put it — to enjoy.

Judith Viorst

Sailing Boats

Frank-Myers Boggs
(Springfield, Ohio 1855-Meudon, 1926)

RIDING THE WAVES

*J*ust as I would navigate a boat to avoid choppy waters, I will not steer myself straight into the waves in our relationship. When the sea is rough, I will turn my motor off and focus on staying afloat, I will ride it out, knowing that I may end up in a different place from where I started. Life is like riding a boat on a changing sea. I am my own boat and I can do what is sane and sensible. Resisting the inevitable flow of the water is neither wise nor prudent. Knowing when to just stay in the boat without rowing and float takes as much dynamic energy as covering vast distances. There are days for traveling and days for riding the waves. I cannot control the sea but I can navigate it. To understand when to act and when to remain still is to meet life on its own terms. To know in our relationship when to act and when to let it be is to live with the potential for grace and wisdom to enter our lives.

Love seems the swiftest, but it is the
slowest of all growths. No man or woman really knows
what perfect love is until they have been
married a quarter of a century.

Mark Twain

SCRUTINY

Everything you do need not meet my scrutiny. If I tried to squeeze you into a shape that meets my approval I would be cheating both of us. I would lose the real you and you would be giving up your real self for an image in a mirror. I will not ask you to take that flight from yourself. Your soul belongs to you. When I try to get you to be who I want you to be, I rob you of your dearest possession — your essential self.

Come live with me and be my love,
And we will all the pleasures prove
That valleys, groves, hills and fields,
Woods or steepie mountains yields.

The shepherd's swains shall dance and sing
For thy delight each May morning:
If these delights thy mind may move,
Then live with me and be my love.

Christopher Marlowe

CONSCIOUS LIVING

*O*ur partnership is unique. Our needs, desires, likes and dislikes are particular to us. I wish to create a safe space in which to understand and express my own uniqueness and allow that same experience for my partner. The sense of safety and security we give each other supports me in moving into life with love in my heart.

My life is what I make of it. I will enter my day with a plan of action. When I wake up in the morning, I will mentally organize the hours that lie before me. It is possible to squander time, for what is life but time? What is the gift of a new day but the gift of twenty-four hours? Why should I let those twenty-four hours pass unnoticed? Why should I be an unconscious person walking around in a semi-fog? It doesn't matter what I do, it matters how I do it. Everything is important when I allow myself to bring my full consciousness to it. It is not what I do but how much awareness I bring to what I do that changes the quality of my life.

The world is so magical that it gives us a direct shock.
It is not like sitting back in our theater chair and being entertained
by the fabulous world happening on the screen. It does not
work that way. Instead it is a mutual process of opening
between the practitioner (person) and the world.

Chogyam Trungpa

ENVY

When I am envious of something that someone else has, such as money, youth, success or whatever, I will ask myself, "Am I jealous of the object/experience or what I imagine that object/experience could give to me?" If I feel that I must be rich, famous or successful in order to be entitled to happiness or a self, that happiness and self are somehow lodged in those things, then I will be jealous of anyone who possesses a piece of my "self," my "happiness." I will be making my culture's icons into my inner gods and I will ever be a slave to them. It is not the possession of these things that will liberate me, but my recognition of where my true sense of self and connectedness really comes from, and that is within. The relationship that I have with my higher self and the people in my life is what nourishes me day to day. My bank account can provide me with many important things, but it cannot buy me life or love or friendship. When I place what I have before who I am, I isolate myself in a well-appointed stylish jail. I will choose life.

It is not love that is blind but jealousy.

Lawrence Durrell

SEEING PERFECTION IN WHAT IS

I will learn to see perfection in things as they are. Beauty always surrounds me if I can let go of my preconceptions of what it should look like. The very act of attempting to control that which lies outside of me dissipates the fullness of the moment because it disallows spontaneity and life. The presence of higher consciousness is in every moment if I can relax and allow it to be there. As I move along in my life, I learn that it is not so much what continues to accumulate around me, but my ability to appreciate what I already have in my life that nurtures my spirit. It takes a healthy body to navigate the world, but it takes a healthy spirit to appreciate and enjoy it. It is the union between what I bring as the observer and that which I observe that creates beauty.

I remember the rage I used to feel when a prediction went awry.
I could have shouted at the subjects, "Behave, damn you,
behave as you ought!" Eventually I realized that the
subjects were always right. It was I who was wrong.
I had made a bad prediction.

B. F. Skinner

MY PRIME

I can take myself lightly. Each day that I look in the mirror, I see that I am losing my race against time just a little. If what is on my face is all that I value, I will also lose my self-acceptance and love just a little each day. I am not larger than nature. I am subject to a life cycle just like anything else. I will not rob myself of my own time simply because I am not "in my prime"; instead, I will redefine what I mean by prime. Prime is a state of my awareness of being. It is my ability to look to a day without anxiety or expectation, willing to see it anew, to experience it as if it had never happened before. Prime is when I can see not what I pretend is there, but what actually is there and appreciate it for what it is. It is when I can live on peaceful terms with life, not constantly looking to it for what it can give to me but wondering also what I might give to it. Prime is when I know how to value the relationships in my life and take good care of them as well as myself.

If you happen to have a great wart on your nose
or forehead, you cannot help imagining that no one else in
the world has anything else to do but stare at your wart,
laugh at it, and condemn you for it, even though
you have discovered America.

Dostoevsky

118

STAYING WITH IT

I could trade you in. I could re-choose, look for another model, try to improve my lot in a variety of ways. But would I be improving or only exchanging for a different set of problems? Are relationships about placing my original order just right or learning to love and stretch and go beyond what I thought were my natural limits? Who can give me just what I want when I hardly know what that is myself half of the time? How can I ask another person to know me better than I know myself or to want to be with me more than I care to be with me? My life with you is an opportunity for growth — a chance to experience myself not as I wish I were but as I really am. If I embrace it as such, I will recognize that both of us are a process not a product. We can help one another to heal past wounds and become better, fuller people, or we can use our relationship as a dumping ground for all that ails us. The choice is ours.

It is better to get rid of the problem
and keep the person than to get rid of the
person and keep the problem.

Horville Hendrix

ALL THE THINGS YOU ARE

I will look to what cannot be
seen and sense the intrinsic beauty of your presence in my life.
All that you give that is unseen will not go unnoticed, unfelt or
unknown. I will not be fortune's fool and learn too late what
I have. I will know it and appreciate it while it is mine. Life
holds no guarantees. But you are here now, I love you now, I
am fed and held by your love now — this day is ours.

So the little prince, in spite of all the good will
that was inseparable from his love, had soon come to doubt her . . .

"One never ought to listen to flowers.
One should simply look at them and breathe their fragrance.
Mine perfumed all my planet. But I did not know
how to take pleasure in all her grace.
The fact is that I did not know how to understand anything!
I ought to have judged by deeds and not by words.
She cast her fragrance and her radiance over me. I ought never
to have run away from her . . . I ought to have guessed all
the affection that lay behind her poor little stratagems.
Flowers are so inconsistent! But I was too young to
know how to love her . . ."

Antoine de Saint-Exupery

Portrait of Madeleine Ingres

Jean-Auguste-Dominique Ingres
(Paris 1780-1867)

BEING HUMAN

You are not here to live up to my fantasies of romance or to make my life worthwhile. I am not here to satisfy your expectations or give you a reason to live. We each search out our own meaning and build our own inner world. I will share mine with you and will try to be mindful of your inner world so that when you unzip your heart to me, I will walk with awareness into that place. We will not be perfect with one another. We may be insensitive and unaware some of the time. It doesn't mean that we are not right for each other; it only means that we are human.

We have a very crazy concept in our culture
called romantic love. We really still believe what they tell us
in musical comedies, that we look across a crowded room and there we
see those special eyeballs that have been waiting for 20 years.
You are drawn together, you embrace and walk out
into the sunset and never have a problem.
What a shame! When we present ourselves as we are,
you recognize that if you are expecting a relationship to be
a continual honeymoon of perfection you are
going to be disappointed.

Leo F. Buscaglia

FAMILIARITY

You have become so familiar to me, almost as if I have always known you — your movements, your touch, the feel of your skin, the sound of your voice, all so much a part of the fabric of my mind, the well worn image of you. When your moods change, they don't shock me so much any more. There is so little of you that I have not seen. We have worked our way into each other's lives in a manner that goes beyond time. It is hard to imagine life without you. I remember it but the feeling of having you around has enveloped me. I do not choose to think of a life without you today. Your ways are too close to my heart and your presence too dear to me. If you went away, I could pretend in the day not to notice but somewhere in the night I would call out your name. I will live both as if we had a thousand years to spend together and as if our lives (as they do) hang constantly in the balance. This life with you has been worth all the work, the heartache and the pain of misunderstanding. Being with you is enough.

True friendship comes when silence between
two people is comfortable.

Dave Tyson Gentry

D'enfer aux Eaux-Chaudes *Millin-Dupereux, (Paris, c. 1810)*

INNER MYSTERY

I honor the mystery within me. In my very being I am a part of two worlds, the known and the unknown. I am a passage through which life is expressed on this earth — a tunnel into eternity — a channel. Though I do not know from where it comes, I sense that life passes through me and is nurtured and sustained by my very essence. I am a carrier of life. Within me is coded a primal knowledge of how to live and love. I am in touch with a pulse — a rhythm beyond me. I am connected to something great and my place on this earth is sacred. All the mystery that lies inside of me is also in you. Life makes no promises, it holds no guarantees. Though you are real, you also come to me as if from a dream. Our union gives life a quiet sense of grandeur. I don't really know how or where it is we come together, but I am deeply grateful that we do. I experience the beauty of us. I treasure the mystery.

Let us go then, you and I,

When the evening is spread out against the sky

Like a patient etherized upon a table.

. . . Oh, do not ask "What is it?"

Let us go and make our visit.

T. S. Eliot

Picture Credits

Thanks to Brandt Dayton & Co., Limited, New York, for the pictures in this book.

Cover picture courtesy of Robin Hubbard.